Grade 1
Reading
Comprehension

Introduction

Reading is the most important skill that your child needs to develop. A child who can read is a child who can succeed. By the time your child completes first grade he or she should be able to read first grade books accurately and with expression. Consistent practice is essential.

This workbook provides your child with the opportunity to read, think and respond; building competence necessary for academic success and life-long benefits.

Contents

How to Use this Workbook

Step 1 - Read the story on the odd numbered page and answer the comprehension questions.
Step 2 - Complete the increased engagement on the even numbered page.

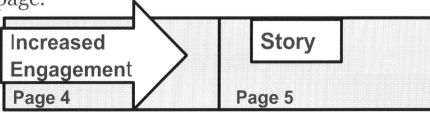

Increased Engagement

In the story "My Prayers" we learn that some people pray at night. What are some things that you do at night before bed?

_____

_____

_____

_____

_____

_____

Name _____

My Prayers

At night I say prayers. I pray because I am thankful for my family. My family takes care of me. I have food to eat, clothes to wear, and a place to live.

1. What do I do at night?

2. Why am I thankful?

3. What does my family do?

4. What do I have?

Increased Engagement

Design a book cover that shows something you like to read about. Color it with crayons or colored pencils.

Name_____

Pam and the Birds

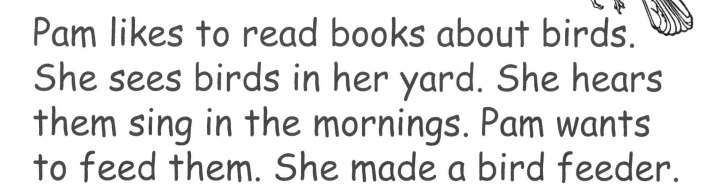

Pam likes to read books about birds. She sees birds in her yard. She hears them sing in the mornings. Pam wants to feed them. She made a bird feeder.

1. What does Pam like to read about?

2. Where does Pam see birds?

3. What do the birds do in the mornings?

4. Why did Pam make a bird feeder?

Increased Engagement

Do you have any sisters or brothers? If so, what do you like to do together? If not, what do you like to do with your parents?

_____

_____

_____

_____

_____

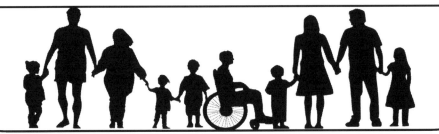

My Baby Sister

I have a baby sister. Her name
is Mia. She likes to crawl around
on the floor. She laughs when I
play peek-a-boo with her. I like
playing with my baby sister.

1. What is my baby sister's name?

2. What does she like to do?

3. When does she laugh?

4. What do I like to do?

Increased Engagement

Draw a picture of something you like to do in hot sunny weather. Color it. Write a sentence about it.

The Sun

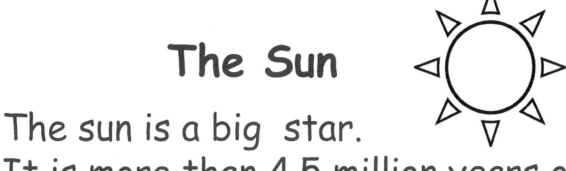

The sun is a big star.
It is more than 4.5 million years old.
It is the closest star to the earth.
The sun gives us heat and light. The
sun helps plants grow.

1. What is the sun?

2. How old is the sun?

3. What does the sun give us?

4. Why do plants need the sun?

Write about one of your favorite birthday experiences. What did you do? What presents did you get? Did you have cake?

_____

_____

_____

_____

_____

_____

Sam's Birthday

Today is Sam's 12th birthday. His birthday present is a blue bike. Sam's favorite color is blue. He likes the bike.

1. How old is Sam?

2. What did Sam get for his birthday?

3. What is Sam's favorite color?

4. Does Sam like his present?

Increased Engagement

Have you ever gone to the zoo?
What is your favorite zoo animal? Why?

Name ——————————

The Zoo

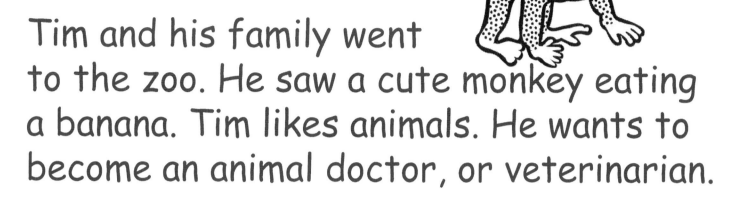

Tim and his family went to the zoo. He saw a cute monkey eating a banana. Tim likes animals. He wants to become an animal doctor, or veterinarian.

1. Where did Tim go?

2. What animal did he see?

3. What was the animal eating?

4. What does Tim want to become?

Increased Engagement

Do cats make better pets than dogs? Why or why not?

PET SHOP

_____

_____

_____

_____

_____

_____

Name ———————————

Meg the Cat

Meg is a little cat. Today she saw a big white dog. The dog started to bark. Meg was scared. Meg ran up a tall tree.

1. Who is Meg?

2. What did she see today?

3. Why was Meg scared?

4. What did she do?

How many stars and stripes are on the United States flag? What do they represent?

_____

There are _____ stars.

_____

The stars represent

_____

There are _____ stripes.

_____

The stripes represent

_____

America

America is a big country. The people come from around the world. They can speak many languages in America. English is the most common.

1. Is America big or small?

2. Where do the people come from?

3. What can the people do?

4. What is the most common language?

Increased Engagement

Draw a picture that shows how you get to school; or homeschool.
Write a sentence for your picture.

Name ————————————————————

Missing the Bus

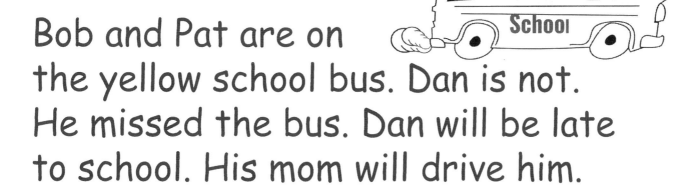

Bob and Pat are on the yellow school bus. Dan is not. He missed the bus. Dan will be late to school. His mom will drive him.

1. What color is the school bus?

2. Who missed the school bus?

3. Where are Bob and Pat?

4. How will Dan get to school?

Jen and her family celebrate Thanksgiving. What is something that you celebrate? Do you eat special foods at that time?

_____

_____

_____

_____

_____

_____

Thanksgiving

Jen and her family celebrate Thanksgiving. They eat roasted turkey, sweet potatoes and apple pie. The food tastes delicious. Jen and her family feel happy and thankful.

1. What does Jen and her family Celebrate?

2. What foods do they eat?

3. How does the food taste?

4. How does Jen and her family feel?

Kim's grandma gave her a puppy as a gift. What is a nice gift that you once received? Who gave it to you? What was the occasion?

_____

_____

_____

_____

_____

_____

Kim's Puppy

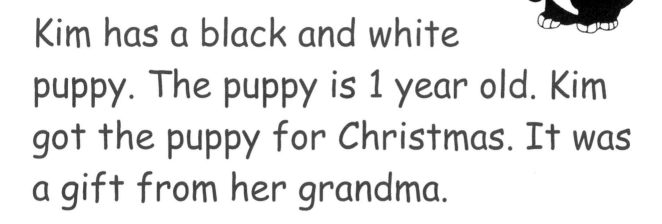

Kim has a black and white puppy. The puppy is 1 year old. Kim got the puppy for Christmas. It was a gift from her grandma.

1. What does Kim have?

2. What color is Kim's Puppy?

3. Who gave Kim the puppy?

4. When did Kim get the puppy?

Increased Engagement

Do you like ice cream?
What is your favorite flavor?

Draw a picture of yourself eating ice cream.

Name _____

Ice Cream

Ann feels hot. She wants chocolate ice cream. Dad buys some for her. It is delicious and cold. Ann loves to eat ice cream.

1. How does Ann feel?

2. What does Ann want?

3. Who buys ice cream?

4. How does it taste?

Increased Engagement

Do you live on a farm? If yes, write about it. If no, do you think you would like living on a farm? Why or why not?

_____

_____

_____

_____

_____

_____

Name ―――――――――――――

The Farm

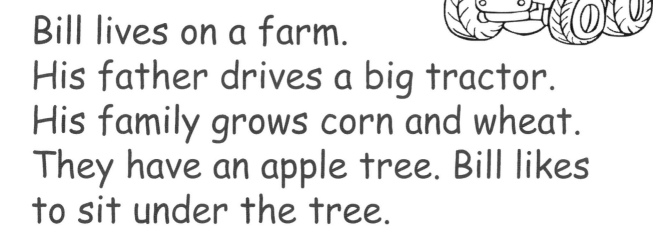

Bill lives on a farm.
His father drives a big tractor.
His family grows corn and wheat.
They have an apple tree. Bill likes
to sit under the tree.

1. Where does Bill live?

2. Who drives a tractor?

3. What do they grow?

4. Where does Bill like to sit?

Increased Engagement

Draw a picture of a tasty lunch. Color your picture.

Pizza for Lunch

Tom had pizza for lunch.
He ate three slices. Tom likes
cheese and mushrooms on pizza.
Pizza is Tom's favorite food.

1. What did Tom eat for lunch?

2. How much did Tom eat?

3. What does Tom like on his pizza?

4. Is pizza Tom's favorite food?

Little Duck wants to catch a fish. Do you know how to fish? Have you ever gone fishing? If not, would you like to go?

_____

_____

_____

_____

_____

_____

The Little Duck

It is a sunny day. Little duck goes to the pond. He splashes in the water. He wants to catch a fish. He has fun in the sun.

1. How is the weather today?

2. Where does little duck go?

3. What does he do in the water?

4. What does little duck want?

Increased Engagement →

What is a good breakfast?

Do you eat soup for breakfast sometimes?   YES ☐ NO ☐

Do you eat toast for breakfast sometimes?   YES ☐ NO ☐

Do you eat eggs for breakfast sometimes   YES ☐ NO ☐

Do you eat rice for breakfast sometimes?   YES ☐ NO ☐

Do you eat oatmeal for breakfast sometimes?   YES ☐ NO ☐

What do you usually eat for breakfast?

I usually eat _____

A Good Breakfast

Did you eat breakfast? It is the most important meal of the day. Breakfast gives you energy. It helps you stay healthy. Warm vegetable soup is good to eat for breakfast.

1. What is the most important meal?

2. What does breakfast give you?

3. How can you stay healthy?

4. What is good for breakfast?

Increased Engagement

Draw a picture of your favorite vegetable.

Draw a picture of your favorite fruit.

Kai the Vegetarian

Kai is a vegetarian. This means that she eats lots of vegetables and fruits. Kai does not eat meat. The doctor says Kai is very healthy.

1. What is Kai?

2. What does she eat?

3. Does Kai eat meat?

4. What does the doctor say?

Write about someone in your family who you think is amazing. What are some things you like about this person?

_____

_____

_____

_____

_____

_____

Name _____

Amazing Grandma

Jay loves Grandma. He thinks she is amazing. Grandma takes him for walks in the park. She tells him funny stories. Jay likes spending time with her.

1. Who loves Grandma?

2. What does Jay think of Grandma?

3. Where does Grandma take Jay?

4. What does Grandma tell him?

Increased Engagement

Have you ever been the new kid? How did that feel? If not, tell what you think it would feel like to be the new kid? Why?

_____

_____

_____

_____

_____

_____

Name _____

The New Kid

Our class has a new kid. His name is Juan. He is from Mexico. He does not speak English. He speaks Spanish. We will help him learn English.

1. What is the name of the new kid?

2. Where is he from?

3. What language does he speak?

4. How will we help him?

Increased Engagement

Write about an outdoor game, sport or activity that you like to do?

_____

_____

_____

_____

_____

_____

My Friend Eli

I have a best friend. His name is Eli. We play an old game called blind man's bluff. On Fridays we watch movies with his dad. On Saturdays we go skating.

1. Who is my best friend?

2. What game do we play?

3. What do we do on Fridays

4. What do we do on Saturdays?

Draw a tree next to the house. Draw a sun in the sky. Color all the pictures.

Trees are Important

Trees give us fruit like apples and oranges. Trees provide shelter for birds and squirrels. We use wood from trees to make furniture. We need to plant more trees.

1. What do trees give us?

2. What do trees provide for animals?

3. How do we make furniture?

4. What do we need to do?

Increased Engagement

Create a habitat with a frog, turtle, or snake in this terrarium.

Don's Pet

Don has a pet frog. He keeps it in a terrarium. His frog eats crickets and climbs on small branches. Frogs can live up to 15 years. Don will have his pet frog for a long time.

1. What kind of pet does Don have?

2. Where does he keep it?

3. What does it eat?

4. How long can frogs live?

Increased Engagement

Does your family have an edible garden? If yes, write about it. If no, is it a good idea for people to grow a vegetable garden in their yards? Why or why not?

_____

_____

_____

_____

_____

Name _____

Backyard Garden

Aunt Sally planted a garden. Roy saw it when he went to visit on spring vacation. The garden had flowers, tomatoes and squash. Aunt Sally likes working in her backyard garden.

1. What did Aunt Sally do?

2. When did Roy visit Aunt Sally?

3. What was in the garden?

4. What does Aunt Sally like to do?

Color each butterfly. Then use the word butterfly in a sentence.

_____

_____

_____

Monarch Butterflies

Monarch butterflies are most familiar. They migrate to warm climates in the winter. They return to the north in the spring. They can fly up to 30 miles an hour and travel up to 100 miles in a day.

1. What happens in the winter?

2. What happens in the spring?

3. How fast can Monarch butterflies fly?

4. How far can they travel in a day?

Increased Engagement

What do you like to do? Draw a picture and write a sentence about it.

Name _____

I Like to Read

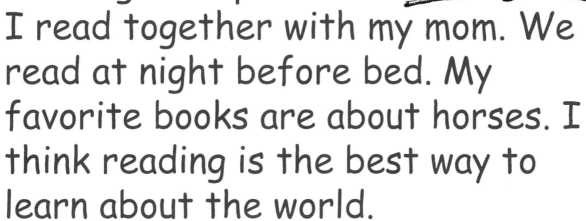

Reading is important. I read together with my mom. We read at night before bed. My favorite books are about horses. I think reading is the best way to learn about the world.

1. Who do I read with?

2. When do we read?

3. What kind of books do I like?

4. What do I think about reading?

What type of schooling do you participate in? What's the best part? What's your least favorite part?

_____

_____

_____

_____

_____

_____

Homeschool is Cool

I like homeschool because I Can learn at my own pace. My parents teach me a lot of things. The best thing is no homework. I eat lunch when I feel hungry. I take a break when I feel tired. Homeschool is good for me.

1. Why do I like homeschool?

2. Who teaches me?

3. What's the best thing about it?

4. When do I take breaks?

Have you been to an amusement park? Beach? Camping? Write about one of your experiences.

_____

_____

_____

_____

_____

Name —————————————————

Amusement Parks

Last summer my family and I went to an amusement park in Florida. We had a lot of fun. The best part was riding the roller coaster.

1. Where is the amusement park?

2. When did I go?

3. Who went with me?

4. What was the best part?

Increased Engagement

Where would you like to travel to? How would you get there?

_____

_____

_____

_____

_____

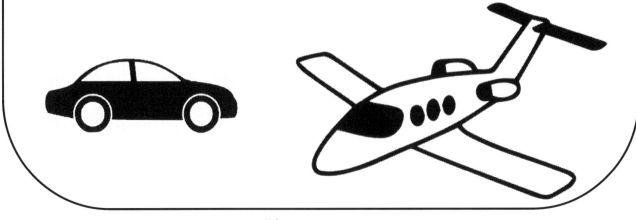

Name ——————————

Statue of Liberty

The Statue of Liberty stands for freedom. It was a gift to the United States from France. It is located in New York. Many visitors travel there to see it.

1. What does the Statue of Liberty stand for?

2. Where did it come from?

3. Where is the Statue of Liberty located?

4. Who travels to see it?

Answers

Name _____

Pam and the Birds

Pam likes to read books about birds. She sees birds in her yard. She hears them sing in the morning. Pam wants to feed them. She made a bird feeder.

1. What does Pam like to read about?

Pam likes to read about birds.

2. Where does Pam see birds?

She sees birds in her yard.

3. What do the birds do in the morning?

The birds sing in the morning.

4. Why did Pam make a bird feeder?

Pam wants to feed the birds.

Name _____

My Prayers

At night I say prayers. I pray because I am thankful for my family. My family takes care of me. I have food to eat, clothes to wear, and a place to live.

1. What do I do at night?

At night I say my prayers.

2. Why am I thankful?

I am thankful for my family.

3. What does my family do?

My family takes care of me.

4. What do I have?

I have food, clothes and a place to live.

Name _____

My Baby Sister

I have a baby sister. Her name is Mia. She likes to crawl around on the floor. She laughs when I play peek-a-boo with her. I like playing with my baby sister.

1. What is my baby sister's name?

Her name is Mia.

2. What does she like to do?

She likes to crawl around on the floor.

3. When does she laugh?

She laughs when I play peek-a-boo with her.

4. What do I like to do?

I like playing with my baby sister.

Name _____

The Sun

The sun is a big star. It is more than 4.5 million years old. It is the closest star to the earth. The sun gives us heat and light. The sun helps plants grow.

1. What is the sun?

The sun is a big star.

2. How old is the sun?

It is more than 4.5 million years old.

3. What does the sun give us?

It gives us heat and light.

4. Why do plants need the sun?

The sun helps plants grow.

Name _____

Sam's Birthday

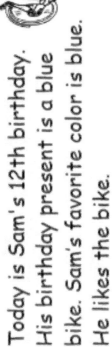

Today is Sam's 12th birthday. His birthday present is a blue bike. Sam's favorite color is blue. He likes the bike.

1. How old is Sam?

Sam is 12 years old.

2. What did Sam get for his birthday?

Sam got a bicycle.

3. What is Sam's favorite color?

His favorite color is blue.

4. Does Sam like his present?

Yes. Sam likes the bike.

Name _____

The Zoo

Tim and his family went to the zoo. He saw a cute monkey eating a banana. Tim likes animals. He wants to become an animal doctor, or veterinarian.

1. Where did Tim go?

He went to the zoo.

2. What animal did he see?

He saw a cute monkey.

3. What was the animal eating?

The monkey was eating a banana.

4. What does Tim want to become?

Tim wants to become a veterinarian.

65

Name _____

Meg the Cat

Meg is a little cat.
Today she saw a big white dog. The dog started to bark. Meg was scared. Meg ran up a tall tree.

1. Who is Meg?

Meg is a little cat.

2. What did she see today?

She saw a big white dog.

3. Why was Meg scared?

Because the dog started to bark.

4. What did she do?

Meg ran up a tall tree.

Name _____

America

America is a big country.
The people came from around the world. They can speak many languages in America. English is the most common.

1. Is America big or small?

America is big.

2. Where do the people come from?

They come from around the world.

3. What can the people do?

They can speak many languages.

4. What is the most common language?

English is the most common.

Name _____

Missing the Bus

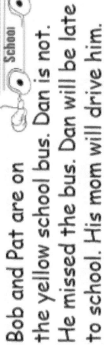

Bob and Pat are on the yellow school bus. Dan is not. He missed the bus. Dan will be late to school. His mom will drive him.

1. What color is the school bus?

The school bus is yellow.

2. Who missed the school bus?

Dan missed the bus.

3. Where are Bob and Pat?

They are on the school bus.

4. How will Dan get to school?

His mom will drive him to school.

Name _____

Thanksgiving

Jen and her family celebrate Thanksgiving. They eat roasted turkey, sweet potatoes and apple pie. The food tastes delicious. Jen and her family feel happy and thankful.

1. What does Jen and her family Celebrate?

Thanksgiving

2. What foods do they eat?

Turkey, sweet potatoes, apple pie.

3. How does the food taste?

Delicious

4. How does Jen and her family feel?

Happy and thankful

67

Name _____

Kim's Puppy

Kim has a black and white Puppy. The puppy is 1 year old. Kim got the puppy for Christmas. It was a gift from her grandma.

1. What does Kim have?

Kim has a puppy.

2. What color is Kim's Puppy?

It is black and white.

3. Who gave Kim the puppy?

Her grandma gave it to her.

4. When did Kim get the puppy?

She got it at Christmas.

Name _____

Ice Cream

Ann feels hot. She wants chocolate ice cream. Dad buys some for her. It is delicious and cold. Ann loves to eat ice cream.

1. How does Ann feel?

Ann feels hot.

2. What does Ann want?

She wants chocolate ice cream.

3. Who buys ice cream?

Her dad buys the ice cream.

4. How does it taste?

It tastes delicious and cold.

Name _____

The Farm

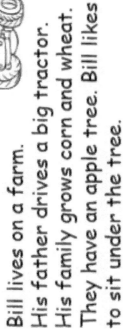

Bill lives on a farm.
His father drives a big tractor.
His family grows corn and wheat.
They have an apple tree. Bill likes
to sit under the tree.

1. Where does Bill live?

He lives on a farm.

2. Who drives a tractor?

Bill's father drives a tractor.

3. What do they grow?

They grown corn and wheat.

4. Where does Bill like to sit?

Bill likes to sit under the tree.

Name _____

Pizza for Lunch

Tom had pizza for lunch.
He ate three slices. Tom likes
cheese and mushrooms on pizza.
Pizza is Tom's favorite food.

1. What did Tom eat for lunch?

Tom ate pizza.

2. How much did Tom eat?

He ate 3 slices.

3. What does Tom like on his pizza?

Tom likes cheese and mushrooms.

4. Is pizza Tom's favorite food?

Yes.

Name _____

The Little Duck

It is a sunny day. Little duck goes to the pond. He splashes in the water. He wants to catch a fish. He has fun in the sun.

1. How is the weather today?

It is sunny.

2. Where does little duck go?

He goes to the pond.

3. What does he do in the water?

He splashes in the water.

4. What does little duck want?

He wants to catch a fish.

Name _____

A Good Breakfast

Did you eat breakfast? It is the most important meal of the day. Breakfast gives you energy. It helps you stay healthy. Warm vegetable soup is good to eat for breakfast.

1. What is the most important meal?

Breakfast

2. What does breakfast give you?

It gives you energy

3. How can you stay healthy?

By eating breakfast

4. What is good for breakfast?

Warm vegetable soup

70

Name _____

Kai the Vegetarian

Kai is a vegetarian. This means that she eats lots of vegetables and fruits. Kai does not eat meat. The doctor says Kai is very healthy.

1. What is Kai?

Kai is a vegetarian.

2. What does she eat?

Vegetables and fruits.

3. Does Kai eat meat?

No

4. What does the doctor say?

The doctor says Kai is very healthy.

Name _____

Amazing Grandma

Jay loves Grandma. He thinks she is amazing. Grandma takes him for walks in the park. She tells him funny stories. Jay likes spending time with her.

1. Who loves Grandma?

Jay loves Grandma.

2. What does Jay think of Grandma?

He thinks she is amazing.

3. Where does Grandma take Jay?

Grandma takes him for walks in the park.

4. What does Grandma tell him?

She tells him funny stories.

71

The New Kid

Our class has a new kid. His name is Juan. He is from Mexico. He does not speak English. He speaks Spanish. We will help him learn English.

1. What is the name of the new kid?

His name is Juan.

2. Where is he from?

He is from Mexico.

3. What language does he speak?

He speaks Spanish.

4. How will we help him?

We will help him learn English.

My Friend Eli

I have a best friend. His name is Eli. We play an old game called blind man's bluff. On Fridays we watch movies with his dad. On Saturdays we go skating.

1. Who is my best friend?

Eli is my best friend.

2. What game do we play?

We play blind man's bluff.

3. What do we do on Fridays

We watch movies with is dad.

4. What do we do on Saturdays?

We go skating.

Name _____

Trees are Important

Trees give us fruit like apples and oranges. Trees provide shelter for birds and squirrels. We use wood from trees to make furniture. We need to plant more trees.

1. What do trees give us?

Fruit like apples and oranges.

2. What do trees provide for animals?

Trees provide shelter for animals.

3. How do we make furniture?

We use wood from trees.

4. What do we need to do?

We need to plant more trees.

Name _____

Don's Pet

Don has a pet frog. He keeps it in a terrarium. His frog eats crickets and climbs on small branches. Frogs can live up to 15 years. Don will have his pet frog for a long time.

1. What kind of pet does Don have?

Don has a frog.

2. Where does he keep it?

In a terrarium.

3. What does it eat?

It eats crickets.

4. How long can frogs live?

Frogs can live up to 15 years.

Monarch Butterflies

Monarch butterflies are most familiar. They migrate to warm climates in the winter. They return to the north in the spring. They can fly up to 30 miles an hour and travel up to 100 miles in a day.

1. What happens in the winter?

They migrate to warm climates.

2. What happens in the spring?

The return to the north.

3. How fast can Monarch butterflies fly?

Up to 30 miles an hour

4. How far can they travel in a day?

Up to 100 miles.

Backyard Garden

Aunt Sally planted a garden. Roy saw it when he went to visit on spring vacation. The garden had flowers, tomatoes and squash. Aunt Sally likes working in her backyard garden.

1. What did Aunt Sally do?

She planted a garden.

2. When did Roy visit Aunt Sally?

On spring vacation

3. What was in the garden?

Flowers, tomatoes, squash

4. What does Aunt Sally like to do?

She likes working in her garden.

Name _____

I Like to Read

Reading is important. I read together with my mom. We read at night before bed. My favorite books are about horses. I think reading is the best way to learn about the world.

1. Who do I read with?

Mom

2. When do we read?

At night before bed

3. What kind of books do I like?

Books about horses

4. What do I think about reading?

I thinks it's the best way to learn about the world

Name _____

Homeschool is Cool

I like homeschool because I Can learn at my own pace. My parents teach me a lot of things. The best thing is no homework. I eat lunch when I feel hungry. I take a break when I feel tired. Homeschool is good for me.

1. Why do I like homeschool?

I can learn at my own pace

2. Who teaches me?

My parents

3. What's the best thing about it?

No homework

4. When do I take breaks?

When I feel tired

Name _____

Amusement Parks

Last summer my Family and I went to an amusement park in Florida. We had a lot of fun. The best part was riding the roller coaster.

1. Where is the amusement park?

In Florida

2. When did I go?

Last summer

3. Who went with me?

My family

4. What was the best part?

Riding the roller coaster

Name _____

Statue of Liberty

The Statue of Liberty stands for freedom. It was a gift to the United States from France. It is located in New York. Many visitors travel there to see it.

1. What does the Statue of Liberty stand for?

It stands for freedom

2. Where did it come from?

It came from France

3. Where is the Statue of Liberty located?

In New York

4. Who travels to see it?

Many visitors

76

The End

Once your children learn to read they will have the power to achieve greatness
~ *Dr. Aleathea R Wiggins*

About the Author

Dr. Aleathea R. Wiggins is a writer specializing in health and education. She is a former university professor, curriculum specialist and teacher.

Dr. Wiggins holds advanced degrees and credentials in journalism, education, health and childcare administration.

Visit Amazon.com to order additional copies of this book.

Please share your family's experience with this book on Amazon.com Reviews.

Recommended reading ~ **"Should My Child Repeat First Grade"** is also available on Amazon.com

Made in United States
Orlando, FL
12 September 2024

51416145R00046